Piece of Me

Mikell L. Murphy

Copyright © 2024 **Mikell Murphy**

All rights reserved. No part of this publication may be reproduced, distributed, or transmitted in any form or by any means, including photocopying, recording, or other electronic or mechanical methods, without the prior written permission of the publisher, except in the case of brief quotations embodied in critical reviews and certain other noncommercial uses permitted by copyright law. For permission requests, write to the publisher, addressed "Attention: Book Rights and Permission," at the address below.

Published in the United States of America

ISBN 978-1-961507-48-7 (SC)
ISBN 978-1-963379-18-1 (SC)

Mikell Murphy
222 West 6th Street
Suite 400, San Pedro, CA, 90731
alaskamd@yahoo.com

Ordering Information and Rights Permission:

Quantity sales. Special discounts might be available on quantity purchases by corporations, associations, and others. For details, contact the publisher at the address above.

For Book Rights Adaptation and other Rights Permission. Call us at toll-free 1-888-945-8513 or send us an email at admin@stellarliterary.com.

CONTENTS

PREFACE v
MY FIRST PUBLIC APPEARANCE 1
DANCING WITH MY STAR 4
KRISTIN AND GOD..7
THE NECESSARY EVIL IN MY LIFE............................10
ALASKA – THEN AND NOW 20
THE MIGHTY CARIBOU HUNTERS 26
MY EARTHQUAKE STORY 30
UP, UP AND AWAY !!..34
DEAR DINGO..38
RING TUM DITTY 42
POEMS: 45
    I SAY ALASKA...45
    MY LEAST FAVORITE TIME OF THE DAY 47
    NO RED HAT, PLEASE...48
    I CARRY MY MOTHER..49
REFLECTIONS IN BLACK AND WHITE.......................51
THE BLUE BUTTERFLY AND MY DEAD FRIEND 55
MY LOST HONEYMOON 58
MY LIFE AS A DRUGGIE 67
MY CREDO..71
MOM WANTED "MORE"..73
DAD'S WORLD VIEW 75
AUNT EUNICE WAS A CLIFFT GIRL 78
PROUD TO BE AN AMERICAN — SORT OF 90

Dad and Mom — 1934

Morn and Dad— 1984

Uncle Allie, the cowboy

Aunt Eunice and uncle Allie -1935

The Cliff girls L to R Maude. Audrey, Burnice mom) Eunice Gladys

PREFACE

The following is a collection of some of my memories, experiences and opinions written through the years of a long and fulfilling life. They certainly do not tell my whole story, but they truly are pieces of it, so I see them as pieces of me. I could not have gathered them together in this little book without the help and encouragement of my husband, David Comins.

MY FIRST PUBLIC APPEARANCE

We had just moved from our home in the oil and dust wasteland of Freer, Texas, to an actual neighborhood in Ft. Worth that summer of 1942. There were no other children nearby, but that did not really bother me. I was five years old and had never really been around other kids anyway.

Then one day a few weeks later, my life changed. Betty Alice Slater, a cousin my age that I had never heard of, and her daddy, a church minister, dropped by. They told us that "Pastor" Slater had been "called" to start a new church right down our street, and we were invited—nay *urged*—to attend services there.

Now Mom had absolutely no use for church. Nevertheless, when she heard that I desperately yearned to go to Vacation Bible School so I could become friends with Cousin Betty Alice, she thought it over and relented. After all, I did suffer from extreme shyness and this experience might help me become a little more socialized.

So off I went with Cousin Betty Alice down the block for a week full of songs and prayers about Heaven and Hell—all new and pretty scary stuff to me but definitely fascinating. I really wanted to fit in with the other children but just didn't know how, so I kept my mouth shut and stayed glued to Cousin Betty Alice.

As the week drew to a close, I learned there was to be something important happening on Friday night. The parents would be coming to Church for a little program put on by the children. Afterward there would be punch and cookies for everyone.

It sounded good to me, and I was definitely up for it until we all gathered together and the teacher started writing down what each child would do for their part in the show. One by one the other children proudly reported what song they would sing or what Bible verse they would recite for everyone. I was shaking with shame—I knew no appropriate song except "Jesus Loves Me," but when I told the teacher that would be my song, she shook her head. "No Honey. We'll all sing "Jesus Loves Me" together as a group"

Having no fallback plan, I blurted out in desperation, "But I can sing it in Chinese!"

I'm sure that little lady's eyebrows went up in disbelief, but there was no one handy for her to check with, and time was getting short, so that became my part of the program.

I am not sure exactly where I got the Chinese idea, but I do know that this was during World War II, and we were urged each mealtime to eat everything on our plates or else we would somehow be hurting all the little hungry children in China.

I was so happy to be part of something that sounded important! I could hardly wait for evening to come so the show could begin. I kept my song a secret from everyone at home. They were going to be so surprised when I got up and sang a song all by myself! O yeah!!

Evening arrived and Mom dressed us in our Sunday best. Dad, the church-loving parent, walked proudly with us down to his Cousin Slater's new little church for its first ever Vacation Bible School program.

Things went pretty smoothly for a non-rehearsed children's event until it was my turn. By then I was pretty sure I had made a dumb decision about my choice of what to do, but it was too late to turn back. The teacher announced that I would be singing "Jesus Loves Me" in Chinese. As I stepped forward, I saw Mom's eyes pop wide open, but the piano lady had started so I started too —in my version of Chinese.

It has been many years since that evening, but I seem to remember it went a little like this: "WING WONG DING DONG LOO LOO LAH. CHING CHING CHONG CHONG WAH WAH WAH". And on like that until the piano lady mercifully stopped playing. I don't remember much about the rest of the show, but I do remember we didn't stay for the punch and cookies. And I do recall how on the way home Mom kept muttering that phrase we were to hear so many other times through the years: "I've never been so humiliated in my life!"

DANCING WITH MY STAR

Dave and I are not very good dancers, but please don't tell us that. We just enjoy ourselves too much to want to hear any criticism about our dancing style. We love to sway together in our own smooth style across the dance floor, or the kitchen floor, or anywhere we might happen to be when the music strikes up our kind of song.

It wasn't always like this, however. On our first dancing date all those years ago I was totally bumfuzzled by whatever it was Dave was doing. His feet and legs were jerking around and his head was bobbing up and down like a puppet on strings.

Now I was considered a really good dancer. I could follow any partner who moved to the beat of the music, but there was no hope of following this herky-jerky style of Dave's. That didn't seem to bother him though. He was in his own zone skittering around in little circles and occasionally grabbing my hand and twirling me under his arm or sometimes spinning himself around undermine.

I had been brought up with music and dancing—all kinds of dancing—but this was new stuff to me, and I did not like it. I came right out and told him, "Listen, I can't dance with you if you won't follow the beat of the music."

Dave was stunned. He thought his fancy footwork was something to be admired, and he had no idea what a "beat" was when talking about music. While I had grown up with piano lessons along with tap and ballet classes, he had only experienced fishing, football, baseball, and wrestling – lots of wrestling. He had absolutely no idea what I was asking him to do.

But Dave is a wonderful man and wanted to please me, so we began taking dance lessons together. His twirling technique and the way he kept trying to spin me under his arm and behind his back most closely resembled the old jitterbug movies, so I signed us up for a swing dance class. My dreams of waltzing in the moonlight would have to wait.

We had lots of fun, and Dave learned all the swing steps and patterns, but he just could not seem to do them to the beat of the music. Oh well, he was getting more predictable and I was learning how to stay out of the way of his flying feet, so we were happy to go to the big dance at the Elks Club at the end of our lesson series.

When we arrived that evening, we were surprised at the number of other folks there who had obviously also been taking swing dance lessons. They really knew how to swing! They knew all the steps we had sort of learned and how to move all around the floor – together! We had thought we were pretty good, but now we hugged the wall like shy junior high kids, afraid to get out there and show ourselves up in front of everyone.

But after a while we did notice another couple who was even worse than we were. The man knew all the steps but went through them in a stiff and wooden way. His partner just did her best to follow along. He obviously never had been taught about dancing to the beat and did not know any more about music than Dave did. We watched awhile, smiling to ourselves, as he stepped mechanically around the floor occasionally bumping into other people but having himself a great time. His long-suffering partner kept smiling gamely and returned to the floor with him dance after dance.

Finally, Dave could stand it no longer. His competitive spirit was aroused. He knew he could do better than that guy, or at least he figured he would not do any worse. He grabbed my hand and we were off to the dances.

I can't say we were great, or even very good, but at least we were better than the klutzy guy who was still step, step, stepping to the music with no style at all. Yes, at least we had style, we smugly told ourselves. We now knew some real swing moves and Dave was allowing me to keep him on the beat with gentle smacks to his shoulder when he got ahead of the music. We began to relax and to enjoy ourselves and our new skills.

After a bit we noticed the really clumsy dancing man was over at his table preparing to leave. We watched as he went around bidding the others their goodnight. Then he took his partner's arm, bent down and picked up a red-tipped white cane, and began tap-tap-tapping his way toward the door.

Yep, we had spent the evening feeling so superior and proud of ourselves because we could move around a crowded dance floor better than a blind man!

KRISTIN AND GOD

On the way home from church on a snowy December morning, Kristin, our youngest, announced that her teacher in Sunday School that morning had said that God lives in Heaven and that Heaven is up in the sky. Kristin was gazing out the car window as she told us this, and it was easy to see that she had questions about this new information. But of course—Kristin always had questions about anything and everything, so I wasn't surprised when she began trying to get her facts straight about God's living situation.

"If God lives up in the sky in Heaven where is his house?"

"If God's house is up in the sky, then where is the road to it?"

"If God has a car, how does He make it stay up in the sky?"

"If God has a garden up in the sky, how does He get the dirt up there?"

"If God grows potatoes in the sky, how does He keep dirt on them till you dig them up?" (Our garden had produced a bumper potato crop that fall, and the kids had helped me dig them out at harvest time.)

The questions went on and on, and my answers got dumber and dumber and more manufactured.

Kristin was right. The whole idea of living up in the sky just couldn't make sense to a smart, inquisitive four-year-old.

Finally, in frustration, I said, "Kristin, I believe that God lives inside people. We all have a little piece of God in us, and He helps us to be kind and to love each other." Surprisingly that seemed to satisfy her, and the God questions stopped.

Now back in those days I believed that I could be the best mom ever. I wanted to do everything right for my family. I had decided that sugar and sweets were bad for my children, so I banished them from our diet. In our home we ate only healthy, nutritious food. The children were all preschoolers, so I got away with this idea for a few years.

But for now, it was the Christmas season, and we were invited to a holiday open house the same afternoon as Kristin's God interrogation. The tables were loaded with candies and cookies and special desserts. My little sugar-deprived children's eyes lit up at the sight of all those yummy goodies. They headed straight for them and began shoveling in everything they could reach.

"Oh well," I thought to myself, "It's Christmas, so why act like the Grinch. Let them enjoy themselves." And they did! I practically had to drag them away when it was time to leave.

That night, as I was putting Kristin to bed, I said to her, "Well, you certainly did eat a lot of candy today, didn't you!"

She looked up wide-eyed and replied, "O no, Mama, I didn't eat any candy!"

Now, even today as a grown woman Kristin is painfully honest. She never has been able to conceal the truth or even to successfully tell a fib, so I was shocked by her answer.

"But Kristin, I saw you reaching for the fudge and eating lots of other candy too."

"O no, Mama. I didn't eat any candy. I just opened my mouth and put it down to God, and He just kept saying, 'Mmm mmm, Kristin. (Little squeaky voice here). That's good! Can I have another piece?' So, I had to keep on giving Him more and more."

THE NECESSARY EVIL IN MY LIFE

Even though I know little and care even less about them, cars became the necessary evil in my life for many years in the usual way weird stories begin.

Yes, it was a dark and stormy night back in 1959 when two good-looking strange men knocked on the door of the little house on a hill in Anchorage, Alaska, and my two housemates, Rosanne and Mary Nell, also from Texas, happily invited them in. I had only been in Alaska for two days and was still wide-eyed at all the new things happening around me, but I joined them in the invitation. The guys' names were Luther, a dentist, and Jorgen, an oil company cartographer.

They had been living in Anchorage long enough to have worked out a routine. On Sunday nights they went around town to "check out" (their words, not mine) the new school teachers and other women who had arrived that week seeking the high wages and possible adventures that Alaska offered in those years.

So, the party began. It was all great fun and certainly different from anything I had experienced in the no-alcohol counties of Texas where I grew up, but we soon decided that we needed more wine. No problem. Jorgen volunteered to go get more and asked me to go along with him.

I was flattered he picked me and happily followed him outside through the mud to his car which shocked me by being small—very small indeed. I felt a little sorry for the guy, not having enough money to buy a decent-sized automobile, but I squeezed inside and off we roared. For such a little car it sure made lots of engine noise as we drove the short distance to a nearby liquor store! Yes, liquor stores were open on Sundays in Anchorage back then.

Jorgen went inside and quickly returned with a jug of wine. He got back in the car and turned the ignition key, but the car refused to start. That's when my life changed forever.

Jorgen asked apologetically if I would mind hopping out and giving the car a push to get it going. "Why sure," I replied cheerily. And that's what I did.

We got back to the party a few moments later and because Jorgen did not say why we were delayed, I stayed silent too. After all, I did not want to embarrass the poor guy by reporting that I had to push his little bitty car to get it going.

Only later did I learn that his little car was a Porsche, the only one in Alaska at that time.

Four months later I was married to Jorgen and was living in a tiny house in the woods outside of Anchorage and still pushing that cranky little Porsche every Saturday to get it going. During the week we commuted to town in a 1950's era Chevy sedan which Jorgen had bought at an Army surplus auction for $200. It was still painted that ugly shade of army green, but Jorgen intended to re-paint it some nicer color. With that plan in mind, he had removed the grill and all the chrome but had never gotten around to an actual paint job.

It looked truly pathetic for the next four years, but at least it started and stopped without being pushed.

The hood was held down with a bungee cord until one day we were speeding along the Seward Highway, the only road into town, when the bungee cord gave way and the entire hood flew up and smashed into the windshield. Of course, it shattered the glass, but it also folded itself back over the top of the car into a perfect right angle. We had to quickly roll down our windows and stick our heads out to see where we were and where we were going. The highway was only a two-lane paved road with deep ditches on each side and no shoulders to use for pulling off, so it was a dicey situation. When we finally were able to stop and attend to the problem, Jorgen was able to pry the hood off the car roof and force it back into place—mostly. The front two feet of it, however, continued to stubbornly stick straight up even after the bungee cord was re-tied. After that day we drove a truly trashy-looking ugly-colored car that had a smashed windshield and a pig snout on the front of its hood.

And what happened to the Porsche, you ask. Well, after more than a year of pushing it around I declared I was through with that scene. Jorgen then decided he would fix the problem. Each Saturday for weeks afterward he took his little car apart looking for the problem and spreading its parts all over the floor of a warehouse belonging to some kind friends. At last, he decided he not only was unable to fix the Porsche, but also, he could not put it back together. He then piled the parts into boxes, smooth-talked the only other Porsche owner in town, a really nice mechanic, into buying all the parts for a cheap price in exchange for Jorgen buying the mechanic's newer Porsche. Jorgen was a very good smooth talker, and I never saw the old Porsche again.

So, we had our second Porsche. Even though Porsches did not have heaters at that time and we were living in Alaska, we made it work for us by wearing heavy coats and constantly scraping the ice from our breaths off the windshield until one day we hit a rock in the road and something expensive underneath was damaged. No one in Alaska had Porsche parts, so they had to be ordered from the factory in Germany. Months later the parts arrived, were installed, and we were off on a long-delayed drive.

We were barely out of our driveway and still in first gear, when the neighbor's dog, a big German shepherd who had never learned to like Jorgen, ran straight at us and hit us head-on. The dog was killed instantly, the neighbor was sad and furious with us, and the Porsche was left with a perfect German Shepherd face imprinted into its front fender. That told me exactly how flimsy this expensive little excuse for a fancy car really was. We might as well have been riding around in a tuna fish can for all the protection it provided us!

And so, the years passed and the cars came and went. None of them were new but they were each one a "good deal." Recently I tried to list the cars that mysteriously appeared and then disappeared from our driveway. I only came up with seventeen different ones, but I am sure there were more.

In my family the purchase of a new car was a big deal. It was planned and discussed together for a long time until the decision of make and model was finally agreed upon by Mom and Dad, and it always turned out to be a Ford sedan. Jorgen did not have that family history though. He often said how he wished he could have been a used car salesman, so cars came and went during my life with him. And much to Jorgen's irritation I often did not even notice when a different one would be sitting unexpectedly in our garage or driveway, He felt I was never really appropriately appreciative of his efforts to keep me in a suitable car. He seemed unable to grasp that my main requirement for a car was reliability. Nothing else really mattered to me.

During the early 60's we had a series of Jeeps, the old square-shaped Willys brand, the forerunners of Wagoneer, I think. The ones that I remember were all boxy and the same sandy tan color. I could only tell them apart if I noticed that the back window was either divided (newer) or not (older). They certainly did not feel any different as I drove them—they were all rough and noisy.

One busy morning I hurriedly loaded all three kids into the dark green Volvo station wagon I was driving at the time, but when I tried to start it, I realized the gearshift was not where it should be. It was a dark green Volvo station wagon parked in the garage as usual, but this one was an automatic gearshift and not my old familiar stick shift. Nevertheless, it was a comfortable car and I liked it until I began to smell gasoline as I drove. I reported to Jorgen that there must be a small leak in the gas line somewhere that might be dripping onto the exhaust pipe. I wanted it fixed because I considered it to be a danger to me and to all the children I was hauling around. In those days before seat belts and car seats you could pile many kids into your car and just tell them to squeeze together or to sit on top of each other.

Jorgen assured me he had examined the situation and found it to be completely safe and nothing to worry about.

A short time later, however, he went to pick up a babysitter and was gone so long that I got worried and called to ask about him. The babysitter answered and said that Jorgen was really busy right then. He was outside throwing snow onto our car because it was on fire. Sure, enough it burned to a crisp.

Another Volvo I remember had a slight electrical problem that caused its headlights to go out periodically often leaving me driving in the dark with a carload of children. I would have to stop as soon as possible and fiddle with switches on the dashboard until the lights came on again. When I complained about this to Jorgen, he tried to calm me down by reminding me that summer was coming soon and Alaskan summer days lasted so long that there would be no real need for headlights then.

A different car appeared soon after that, but it did not last long either. It seemed the reverse gear would not work so that after it was parked in the garage it had to be pushed out again to go anywhere. And you already know how I feel about that.

Next came our series of Waggoneers, and I really liked them—most of the time. There was the one that was stolen out of the church parking lot while I was busy teaching Vacation Bible School one summer morning. Luckily, it was recovered that same day. I had felt stupid calling the police to report my stolen car because I could not identify it to their satisfaction. I did not know the year or even the correct color (I thought it was dark green, but it was some sort of dark blue instead). Remember, I do not pay much attention to cars as long as they stop and go when needed.

All I could tell the authorities was that it had a contraption on the front of it that I thought was called a "wimp".

Actually, I learned later that it was really a "wench" and was used to pull things out of ditches. But "wimp" was enough of a description that a trooper listening on the police radio while cruising the area recognized our blue/green Wagoneer with some sort of machine on the front of it coming at him on a nearby rural road. The trooper did a U-turn and the chase was on! The two teenagers in our stolen car realized the jig was up, so they opened their doors and bailed out without stopping it. The Wagoneer was left to run off the road and crash into a wooded ditch where it was soon found. The wench was then used to get it out and onto the road again in time to be returned to church just as Vacation Bible School was ending. I piled the kids back into it and drove them home without missing a beat. Later that day I got a phone call from parents asking if our car had really been stolen the way their kids were telling them.

Mechanical problems continued to be my nemesis with cars. I remember another Wagoneer that had a problem with teeth missing from its flywheel. Everything would be just fine until I would stop someplace that would catch the flywheel where some of its teeth were gone. When that happened, the engine could not start. I would have to get out, open the hood, climb up on the front bumper and stand there with one foot up on the edge of the engine compartment so that I could grab the flywheel in both hands and start pulling with all my might to turn it past the section where the teeth were missing. Then I would climb back down, close the hood, get back in the car, start it up and get going again. It doesn't sound so bad, but flywheels are really heavy and hard to turn, plus this was happening in the days of miniskirts. That meant I would be standing up on the bumper bent over the engine compartment with my fanny basically flashing all the cars driving slowly by behind me.

Jorgen also had car problems. He once had a fancy Volvo sports station wagon which he bought as an "investment" and loved to drive, especially since its engine was as loud as a Porsche. One night he called from downtown just at dinnertime. The car would not start. He was parked on the top floor of the city parking garage, and he needed me to come and tow him to get it going. I loaded the hungry kids into the car and drove the 15 miles downtown to the rescue. It was after 6:30, businesses were closed and it was already dark, so downtown was basically deserted and Jorgen's little orange sports car was the only one still parked up there on the roof.

We attached the tow rope so I could pull him till we were going fast enough down the ramp that he could" pop the clutch" and get the engine running. We had done this many times before but only on flat roads and never in a parking garage with a circular drive going down for five floors. I was sensibly nervous, but what's a wife to do when her husband needs her help?

Off we went with me driving as fast as I could go around and around until we got to the street below. Nothing from the Volvo. It was still dead. Jorgen appeared at my car window and said we had to go back up and do it again, but this time I needed to go faster. OK, so I towed him back up to the top floor and down we went –again. This time I was driving really fast down the spiraling ramp to the street. The kids thought we were on a carnival ride – lots of laughing and squealing from the back seat. Me—I was just sweating.

Still not fast enough, Jorgen reported. Next time I just had to go faster. I told him flatly that this next time would be the last time, and he had better get his little car started or else. I do not think he heard me because the next time I went so fast I knew I could not go faster, and when his car still did not start, I just kept driving down the street towing him in it behind me. I did not stop even though I could see him in my rear-view mirror wildly waving his arms at me. I just drove straight to a friend's home not far away, got out, untied the tow rope and turned to face a very angry husband.

"The kids are hungry, and I am not going to keep doing this crazy thing tonight. You can get in and come home with us now, or you can stay here and figure out something different yourself.

We are leaving."

Jorgen got in, and we had a very quiet ride home. The car eventually got home the next day, but I did not ask how.

There are many other stupid stories about my life with cars and the husband who loved them, but I will just tell you one more.

We had a small 18-foot Winnebago that our family used happily for years. We named it the Winnie-B, and in the winter, it sat in our driveway until the snow melted. One year, however, we needed it to go somewhere before winter had ended. Unfortunately, its tires had sunk into the driveway's soft asphalt surface over the winter, and no matter how hard Jorgen gunned the little Winnie B's engine it just could not get the wheels out of those indentations. I was called to come outside and help. The kids and I got into my trusty little Wagoneer (this one was orange, I remember), and the tow rope was attached. Jorgen instructed me to go forward until the rope was taut and then to jerk it hard enough for the RV's wheels to be pulled out of their driveway ruts.

OK, I knew the drill and was ready to jerk as directed. I did as tell, but the little Wagoneer could not dislodge the larger RV. I went back to consult with Jorgen. He told me that I just had to back up a bit more, drive forward faster and then jerk it. I followed those directions carefully and my car actually pulled so hard that our front wheels were lifted off the ground and into the air, but no movement from the RV. Once again, I walked back for another suggestion from Jorgen. He was up higher than I because he stayed at the RV steering wheel while talking to me down on the driveway.

"You just have to put more power into it and really give it a jerk!" He declared.

Again, I went back to my driver's seat, backed up as directed, and told the kids to hang on. Then I put us in gear, hit the gas and plunged ahead with a real jerk. To my surprise it worked! I continued on to the end of the driveway. Then I looked in the rearview mirror and saw that the Winnie B had not moved. Instead, I was dragging its grill, its bumper and its battery through the snow behind me.

I stopped and carefully got out. I slowly walked toward the RV, but when I saw Jorgen's stunned expression up there through the windshield I just had to laugh. In fact, I doubled over laughing because his look of disbelief was so silly. He was staring down at the RV's innards scattered along the driveway. I watched as he slowly stood up, came to the door and opened it. He looked out at me and then said very seriously, "Now look what you've done."

ALASKA – THEN AND NOW

In June, 1959, I was free at last – ready to leave home, go out and conquer the world equipped with my brand-new diploma from Texas Woman's University. I had lots of big ideas about excitement, romance, and earning my own money, but the only job offered me that summer was doing public relations work for TWU. My traveling partner and friend was another TWU graduate who, coincidentally, was also named Mikel (but with just one L). We were the M&M traveling team for TWU. Our job was to drive to various West Texas towns and stage punch-and-cookie parties for high school girls as we tried to convince them to enroll in college before they got married and settled down.

It was hot and dusty work in those days before air-conditioned cars and motel rooms, and our per diem was a measly $5.00 each, so by the time we reached El Paso I was more than ready for the postcard that arrived from Rosanne Keller, another TWU grad. She had headed north for Alaska that summer, and her message was, "COME TO ALASKA! YOU CAN LIVE WITH US. THERE ARE MEN EVERYWHERE!" That postcard ended my public relations career.

Two weeks later I waved good-bye to my bewildered parents and flew to Anchorage, Alaska. It had been an easy decision. The highest-paid teaching job I could get in Texas was in Houston for $3200.00 a year, but Anchorage offered me the splendid sum of $6000.00!

It took two full days to fly there from Ft. Worth in 1959, so I wasn't exactly fresh as a daisy upon arrival, but I perked up when I finally got a look at Anchorage. I had been expecting igloos and snow. Instead, there was a full-sized airport and an actual city with real streets and stores and even a couple of 12-story apartment buildings towering over all the other squatty little buildings in town.

And no igloos or snow either—just lots of drizzle and mud. I had to wait for three full weeks before the clouds lifted and for the first time, I could see that Anchorage is surrounded by tall mountains. That was truly an exciting day for this flatland Texan!

Anchorage in 1959 was a city of less than 80,000 and felt much smaller because there were few places to go or things to do, so we thought we knew everybody. Today the population is around 300,000, and it is becoming more and more difficult to even know the folks in our own neighborhood. Life has become much busier with all the modern options for entertainment and recreation to fill any free time left over from earning the two salaries it generally takes to maintain the large, modern homes that today's couples feel they must have.

Before the Great Alaskan Earthquake in 1964, homes were kept small enough to be affordable to maintain and to heat in a harsh and often destructive climate that could freeze your pipes, crack your foundation, or flood your basement unless you carefully monitored it all year round.

Many people built their own homes. Houses were very expensive, but most builders had all winter off so they had time to work on their own places. That was because the snow that appears on the mountaintops each October was called "termination dust" and signaled the end of the year's construction season. This meant that carpenters and others in the building trades were usually laid off.

This practice continued until the big 1964 Alaska Earthquake which caused so much damage to Southcentral Alaska. Builders were forced to develop different techniques and materials that would allow people to continue working outdoors in frigid temperatures. Today construction goes on around the clock and all year long, thanks to what Alaskans learned that sad and difficult year. Now there are beautiful big homes lining the streets of the subdivisions that seem to spring up from one season to the next.

As in many cities, the hillside areas are where the wealthier folks like to live, but back in 1964 when we built our home on the mountainside it was so far out of town that land was cheap and plentiful. Our home was one of the first on "The Hillside." We joked that the only thing blocking our view was Mt. McKinley over 90 miles north of us. We could stand on downtown streets and point to our red roof clearly visible as one of the few houses up that high. Nowadays there are thousands of homes, several schools, and a honeycomb of roads up on that same hillside.

Where once my teenage son would disappear for hours on his snowmobile, and we could cross country ski, go hiking, or pick berries without seeing other people, there are now huge houses and even a gated community or two. Oldtimers like us have decided that the peace and quiet we enjoyed on "our"

Hillside has been wiped out by too many newcomers, so we have moved down nearer to town to be closer to city life amenities now that Anchorage is indeed a city. However, along with the city's conveniences have come the usual city problems.

Traffic is a serious headache even though nearly all streets are now paved, freeways are available (some with six lanes), and cars can have studded snow tires. When I first began driving in Anchorage, most streets were rough and unpaved. Cars regularly slid off the road into snowbanks. But, never mind, there were not enough other cars on the road to worry about collisions. Besides, the next driver to come along would pull you out, and off you'd go again— with maybe a new dent or two, but no real harm done. That doesn't happen today. If you're lucky enough to land in the ditch without hitting another car first, you had better have your cell phone ready to call a tow truck because it is very unlikely that some stranger will stop and assist you.

In the early 60s we took care of one another. We were young and there were lots of parties with dancing and drinking, but we made sure that everyone got home safely, and during those years I never saw or heard of anyone "doing drugs." Beer and laughter were our drugs of choice, and there were always plenty of those to go around.

Unfortunately, drugs and the crimes that accompany them have reached Alaska and are wreaking havoc among our young people—even those in faraway rural villages where the Eskimos and Indians are caught between their traditional cultures and the modern way of life. Alaska Natives are a large minority in Anchorage, and their numbers are growing as many leave their villages for jobs in the city.

Fifty-six years ago, most folks in Anchorage were Caucasian, and it was fairly unusual to see an Alaska Native there, but today they represent more than 10% of our population. Anchorage is rapidly becoming culturally diverse. Immigrants from the South Pacific Islands, the Philippines, Mexico and other Hispanic countries are moving in greater numbers to Anchorage each year.

Anchorage teachers deal with more than eighty different languages and it is expected that Caucasian students will soon be the minority school population. Immigrants are drawn northward by the increased opportunities for jobs in our growing economy, the very low taxes in Alaska, and the annual Alaska Permanent Fund Dividend checks handed out to each man, woman and child who has lived in Alaska for an entire year.

And who can fault them for that?! Basically, these newcomers leave their homes far behind them and choose Alaska for the same reasons I did—to earn more money and to have a chance to live a better life. Still, there are certain differences in life then and life now which those of us who came before the oil and pipeline booms can point out.

We were looking for more money, yes, but we were also willing to work hard to get it and to put up with some rough living conditions along with isolation and high expenses. We wanted excitement and new experiences and were willing to take risks to get them.

Today, many new arrivals come with the expectation of a comfortable lifestyle with not much extra effort required to have it. They want clothes from Nordstrom's, elegant homes, cars that look new --Alaskan cars of the 60's were sure to be dented and dirty. Their children play hockey with expensive equipment on big heated indoor rinks instead of outdoor rinks on school playgrounds. Teenagers go to high schools with indoor swimming pools. People actually dress up to go to the opera --yes, Anchorage has had its own opera company and symphony for years, but we used to wear anything that kept us warm when we went.

Nowadays it seems to matter what one wears and how one looks. When we arrived a half century ago, we had few concerns about our appearances. Staying warm was the important thing. And you were not judged by what you owned, but by what you could do. It was the kind of classless society that reflects the frontier, and that is gone.

But Anchorage is still surrounded by incredible beauty and filled with interesting people who like to do interesting things, so I still choose to live there at least half of the year—the warmer half! As we tell folks, we live in Anchorage because it is so close to Alaska!

Fifteen minutes from downtown we can be high on a mountain in the wilderness of the nation's largest state park literally across the street from expensive homes. Right out the back door of our midtown condo is a wooded greenbelt with a biking/hiking path that will quickly put us into trees so thick that we have to watch carefully for moose—and sometimes a bear as we walk along. Yet the same bike path will take us on into the city center and on out the other side to miles of scenic shoreline and more wooded parkland. Anchorage has to be experienced to be believed or appreciated!

So why don't I continue to live there all year round? Because I'm tired of the long, dark winters, and because I'm a native Texan and my Daddy used to say, "Every Texan wants to retire and move to the Hill Country." So, I did.

THE MIGHTY CARIBOU HUNTERS

On many snowy mornings in the early 1960s we could hear the local radio announcing, "Caribou herds crossing the highway south of Eureka," or some other location along the road north of Anchorage. This was the signal for hunters to get their guns and head north to shoot enough caribou for their family's winter meat supply.

We were young, new to Alaska, and ready to try anything sounding even vaguely adventurous, so the idea of hunting a caribou seemed like just the thing to do on the next Saturday morning.

Of course, we had never tasted caribou or even seen one, but that did not matter. I had just come up from Texas and my new friends, the Parkers, had arrived a few weeks earlier from Louisiana. Mari was tall and slim while Gordon was short and round. They were school teachers and great companions whenever you wanted to have some laughs or a delicious home-cooked southern meal.

Gordon was sure a caribou steak would taste "mighty fine" after Mari got through with it. Plus, he had a gun! Jorgen Lilliebjerg, my new husband, had grown up in downtown Copenhagen, Denmark, but assured us he knew all about hunting big animals. As a young bride I didn't want to doubt him, so we were good to go.

Our plan was to leave early in the morning, drive north until we saw all those caribou crossing the highway, shoot one for ourselves, tie it on top of the car, and drive right back home to Anchorage for a caribou dinner.

So, the very next Saturday we put on our warmest clothes, spooned a big pot of my spaghetti into our new plastic thermos jug, poured fresh coffee into a smaller thermos, and piled into the Parkers' little red VW bug. We were off to get a caribou!

We four adults barely fit into that little car, and Volkswagens didn't have good heaters back then, so it wasn't exactly a comfy ride. Besides the squeezed-seating arrangement, the road was snowy and slick, so Gordon kept hitting the brakes to see if they actually worked on ice. Each time he did this, we would slide sideways or swerve wildly, and Mari would yell at him to "Stop fooling around and get serious or you'll kill us all!"

We had started before sunrise, but after hours of our erratic driving the sun was up and shining on a beautiful Alaskan day. Soon we began to spot piles of caribou guts left alongside the road by previous hunters who had already shot and skinned their prey. We slowed down, peered out the steamy car windows across snow-covered land in all directions but saw no sign of any caribou.

Just as we almost decided that we had missed the big caribou herd and needed to turn back, there he was! A really big caribou standing out there all alone in a field of snow about 100 yards from the road! O boy! Caribou steak tonight!

With lots of shushing each other and stumbling around, we untangled ourselves from the little car and stood in the road to plan our attack. It was Gordon's gun, so he wanted to carry it, but ten feet off the road the snow was chest deep, so he changed his mind. It was decided that Jorgen, the tallest of the group, should walk first in line, breaking the trail for us and carrying the gun high enough to keep it out of the snow.

Off we trudged, heading straight across the field toward our caribou. He lazily looked our way, tossed his head disdainfully and then ignored us. He didn't even try to hide or run away. He obviously sensed that we were not a serious threat.

We crunched closer until we had covered almost half the distance to our nonchalant target. It began to look as if we could actually get close enough to shoot him. We stopped to discuss the next step of our ragged little plan. That's when reality hit us. We realized we had a few problems to consider:

1. We were already huffing and puffing from struggling through deep, soft snow, but we still had far to go.

2. If we really did manage to kill this big beautiful animal who wasn't bothering anybody, we would then have to keep on slogging through deep snow until we got to him.

3. Then we would have to cut him up and somehow carry him back to the car. That didn't sound like fun at all!

4. And there was another problem: We had a gun, but nothing else—no knife, no tools to skin a dead animal or to cut it up into chunks of meat, and nothing to carry meat in.

This called for a group consultation. Maybe shooting a caribou wasn't such a great idea after all!

In fact, why didn't we just get ourselves on back to the car and head for home? After all, we had that big jug of spaghetti and a thermos of coffee, so why were we standing out in this freezing cold field acting as if we wanted to kill something?

It didn't take more than a few seconds to make our decision. We struggled back to the little car, squished ourselves in again, and turned toward Anchorage, snacking on cold spaghetti and lukewarm coffee all along the way.

But before we reached home, we decided that we had actually been on two different hunts that day–our first one and our last one!

MY EARTHQUAKE STORY

We were living in a very little house in the woods outside of Anchorage with no close neighbors when the Great Alaskan Earthquake struck in 1964. My husband had just returned from taking our rowdy foster child to his mother's home to celebrate his twelfth birthday, and we sat down to enjoy a glass of wine and a rare quiet evening together.

Soon the shaking started, but we were not at all disturbed. After all, these little tremors happened now and then. They lasted a few seconds and were nothing to worry about. But something was wrong this time. The shaking did not stop. Indeed, it went on and on getting stronger and louder until the wine had sloshed completely out of our glasses. Books and dishes were tumbling off their shelves all around us. By that time, we had struggled to our feet, and my husband was shouting over the rumbling and crashing for me to stand in the door frame. Our two beagles were hysterically dashing around the room, and no doorframe on the planet would have seemed safe to me by then. I wanted *out* of there!

The dogs and I rushed outside to the open air and away from the creaks and groans our swaying walls were adding to the uproar. The house was being torn apart, and there was no way I wanted to be inside and under it when it came down!

But once outside and into the cold March evening, the noise and danger were still there. The ground was rippling and heaving so much that we could not stay on our feet. I was thrashing around on my hands and knees in the mud and snow of spring breakup season alternately crawling and staggering down the driveway as fast as I could to get away from the screaming of old planks and nails as they were pulled apart at the corners of the walls and then slammed back together in our little shack of a home. The chimney was alternately leaning away from the house and then smacking back against it. The tall birch trees in the yard were being lashed back and forth so violently they were whipping the ground on either side of me.

From my knees I stared around me seeing only certain ruin. I could hear nothing but the loudest possible roar of some huge and invisible locomotive that would not leave the station—it just kept staying there all around us.

Once or twice the tumult would subside enough for me to scramble to my feet only to start up again, stronger than ever, knocking me back to the ground. "Well," I thought, strangely calm inside, "So this is the end of the world. This is what it feels like to die." I wasn't even afraid, just totally amazed and unprepared for what was happening all around me.

The dogs had long since disappeared into the woods by the time the noise and the shaking began to gradually calm down. And then it ended.

It had been going on for over four minutes! Try standing in front of your clock sometime for that long and imagine yourself in the middle of the roar and shaking of the strongest earthquake ever recorded in North America.

You might get some idea of how I could have truly believed that the world was ending.

But now everything just stopped, and it was quiet again. But it was a quiet that I had never felt so strongly before.

The earth and all that was in it were silent. Nothing moved. The house still looked amazingly intact. The chimney had righted itself with only the top two layers of blocks now sitting askew.

We gingerly re-entered and found a complete and total mess inside.

Everything was thrown to the floor, and our tiny kitchen was awash in the contents of the refrigerator and cabinets. Most disturbing though was the sound of running water coming from the basement. Obviously, the pipes had broken down there, and we needed a plumber fast.

My husband retrieved the phone from wherever it had been thrown and dialed the number for our plumber friend. He had just recently installed new water pipes for us. Amazingly he answered his phone and said he would be right over.

We were all acting absurdly normal—we just did not yet know how else to respond to what had happened. To tell the truth, none of us really *knew* what had happened. It was too much to put into words for now. That phone call was the only one we made that month because local telephones did not work again for weeks.

Rather than face the mess inside, I went out to look for our dogs. Up and down the unnaturally quiet road I walked calling their names. *"Adelaaaaide*! *Ambroose!* It's all right now. You can come home."

No response, and I silently swore never again to name pets such silly names. The dogs came slinking back home much later that night and were jumpy for weeks.

For now, I was all by myself in a world that a little while earlier I had believed was ending forever. Yes, indeed!

I had survived the end of the world! That awareness, combined with the current creepy stillness around me made me feel like a ghost.

Then I was suddenly face to face with a very large moose, just standing in the trees only a few feet in front of me. He looked as confused as I felt. He shook his big woolly head and gave me a look that plainly asked, "Hey, lady, what the heck just happened here?"

"I don't know," I replied, "but I'm going home." I hurried away leaving him staring forlornly after me.

We were busy with the cleanup process when our plumber friend finally arrived much later. "Sorry to take so long," he said, "but the roads are a mess and I had to take a few detours to get here."

That was when it hit us that this earthquake was not just a neighborhood event. "My goodness!" I exclaimed, with no idea of the extent of the damage that had been done to Alaska by this quake. "I wonder if they felt it downtown!"

UP, UP AND AWAY!!

Back in the 1970s we could look up almost any blue-sky day and see brightly-colored hot air balloons floating above Anchorage. How could anyone feel sad when they could watch such pretty shapes and colors bobbing playfully up and down with our majestic Chugach Mountains as their backdrop! Everyone agreed they added a lot of pizzazz to our city. Sadly, however, their liability insurance rates were soon raised so high that the balloon owners were forced to fold their big toys into their oversized wicker passenger baskets and leave Alaska.

But before they left, I was lucky enough to get a ride in one of them, and what a ride it was! My former husband arranged for us to take the "Champagne Special" one very cold day in January. We were scheduled to meet the balloon crew at the Bodenburg Butte, near the little town of Palmer. We were to go up and float around the Butte for an hour, drinking champagne and admiring the view.

When we arrived, the ground crew was already busy laying out the huge rainbow-colored bag in the field so that it could be inflated. Every balloon owner had a "ground crew" to help unpack and to inflate the balloon. Then once the balloon was airborne, the crew would chase along on the ground in a truck so that they were handy when the flight ended and they could put the balloon away. It was a lot of work, but in return for their labor they got free balloon flights. This crew obviously thought it was a good trade-off because they weren't even grumbling about how cold they were as they struggled with the flopping balloon fabric in the sharp wind.

Hot air balloons get their hot air from a propane burner that ignites with a very loud roar and shoots flames up into the balloon cavity until it is full of enough hot air to be lighter than the air outside it and *voila!* it floats up and off the ground. I did not know that basic detail of ballooning, so the first time the burner suddenly roared with flame I was so startled that I jumped away and landed on my back in a snowbank. By the time I was up on my feet and brushed off, the balloon was upright and straining to take off in the wind. The owner had a worried look in his eye as he tossed up a handful of grass and watched it blow away.

"Too windy to fly today," he announced to the groans of his ground crew. "Put her away and we'll try again tomorrow." Reluctantly the young men began to let the air out of their big ball and started refolding it to fit back in its sack.

"But what about our champagne deal?" we asked wistfully.

"Well, just because we can't fly doesn't mean we can't drink champagne, does it?" grinned the owner.

It didn't take long for us, the owner, and his crew to finish off two bottles of the bubbly, and somehow the day seemed warmer when we were done. The owner tossed up another handful of grass, and when it landed nearby, he declared, "Wind's fallen off, boys. Let's fly!"

I was thrilled to be getting my balloon ride after all and felt too buzzed on the champagne to worry about the wind which had definitely not completely "fallen off." The ground crew was also happy and didn't even complain about re-doing all their earlier work getting the balloon unfolded and blown up again. And this time I knew what was happening so that I stayed on my feet and out of the snowbank when the burner roared and the balloon began to fill.

Along with the owner we scrambled into the passenger basket, the weights were tossed out and up we went! Up and up and up we went until we were floating high over the Butte and then higher still over the farms below. The owner was on his little radio trying to give our position to his crew in the truck somewhere below us. They were desperately trying to keep us in sight as we soared higher and farther than anyone had planned. He sounded worried, but I was having a grand time.

Balloon flying is silent! You're actually *in* the wind so you can't feel it or hear it. You're just part of whatever is happening in the sky at that moment, and I loved the sensation. However, our pilot obviously did not. He was trying hard stay calm and to maintain the appearance of being in total control even though it was clear that no one was piloting this baby but the blowing wind.

"I'll just take her down to some quieter air," he said as he fiddled with something that let air out of the balloon and we sank down much closer to the ground. In fact, we feel so low we were bumping along smacking treetops before he decided to hit the burner button and send fire and hot air up into the balloon so that we could go higher again.

Our pilot was now busy on the radio trying to help his crew catch up with us and was muttering about how we should have been equipped with crash helmets. I was having a wonderful ride though and not worrying about a thing until I looked down and saw that we were fast approaching the railroad bridge and the icy waters of the Knik Arm which leads straight to Cook Inlet and then on to the Pacific Ocean.

No more Mr. Calm and Cool Owner. "We've got to get this thing down before we land in the drink!" he said as he started deflating the balloon as fast as possible.

"Put the little one in the front!" he yelled.

Now I'm not actually "little," but I was definitely smaller than the two tall men I was with at the moment, so I got shoved to the front of the basket as we fell rapidly toward the snow below us.

It was not a pretty landing with the wind as strong as it was that day, but as pilots say, "Any landing you walk away from is a good landing." And after being dragged face down through the snow with two big men on top of me, I was able to crawl out of the basket and walk away, so it was definitely a good enough landing as far as I was concerned.

We had come down onto the snowy "flats" between the highway and the railroad tracks, the last level space before the frozen swamp water of Knik Arm.

When I stood up, I saw a long line of cars stopped along the road their passengers clapping and cheering for us. We had evidently put on an impressive show as we had abruptly smashed into the snow and were dragged to a stop right in front of them.

It was a wonderful flight, even if it didn't go as smoothly as planned. I will always be glad that I got to float up in one of those big sky ornaments they call hot air balloons while we had them here with us in Anchorage.

DEAR DINGO

Dear Dingo,

This is just a little letter to tell you that you are absolutely the best dog I ever had. In fact, you are probably the best dog Anybody ever had.

You came to us one snowy morning as I was trying to get all three youngsters dressed to go outside, and that day you changed our lives. You probably didn't know it, but Erik was terrified of dogs—ever since that huge, slobbery St. Bernard knocked him down and rolled him over before I could get to him and set him upright on his little toddler feet. From that moment until you arrived, he would run whimpering away from any dog he saw no matter how we tried to soothe and reassure him. He was just a quivering mess around dogs until that morning when you were tossed out of some car in front of our house.

I had Erik all dressed for the cold and had set him out the front door and was still wrestling Anne-Lise into her coat so she could go out too. I had handed Kristin a cracker to keep her quiet until I could get to her next.

Suddenly we heard Erik pounding on the door right outside. He was screaming something about a dog trying to bite him. I opened the wooden door and immediately saw that you were there with Erik, trying to lick his hand.

You were so small and scrawny that I knew you wouldn't hurt him, and besides I didn't want to start over on undressing and re-dressing the kids for our morning walk outside, so I snatched the cracker away from Kristin and barely cracked open the door so I could hand it out to Erik. Quickly you took it and gobbled it right down. Erik looked down dumbstruck at his hand and saw that it still had all five fingers and was not bleeding. Immediately he turned to me and announced with a four-year-old's authority, "I need another cracker, Mom. My dog is still hungry."

And that was the end of Erik's fear of dogs and the beginning of a beautiful relationship between you and our family and friends and neighbors and anybody who ever came near you.

No one could figure out what kind of dog you were—we knew you looked like a too- small golden retriever, but not really. All we knew was that you were madly in love with us and absolutely fearless when anyone approached us in a threatening way.

Over the years you took on those terrible Doberman Pinschers one crazy neighbor trained as attack dogs and the big German Shepherds at the campground that time and, of course, you protected the kids from the occasional moose who wandered into our yard. And do you remember how you hovered over my sixteen four-year-old preschoolers when I had a playschool at our house? I don't know how you did it, but you kept them all safely away from the road and herded them together into the safe parts of our property while keeping the dogs who ran loose in our neighborhood at a safe distance away from them. You even made sure they did not run into the path of the metal swings when they were in action—and always without barking or growling.

In fact, Dingo, you only barked at squirrels teasing you from their perch up in the trees or at cars driving by. You absolutely could not resist chasing cars, and that drove me crazy. No matter how much I scolded, you chased almost every car driving by. And then you always came creeping up to me so pitifully because you knew you had done wrong. In fact, out of desperation one time I hit you while you were crawling toward me in that guilty way you had when you were apologizing. You rolled onto your back and tried to block my blow with your paw, but instead I struck you and got a little scratch on my hand. I was so ashamed of myself for hitting you! That little scratch left a small scar on my hand that still serves today to remind me not to ever lose my temper or to hit anyone again, even a dog. See what a good teacher you were, Dingo!

We traveled a lot in those days, and you always went with us. You were very frightened of getting into the motor home and would hide in the tall grass as you watched us, we pack for a trip. Then we would have to go find you and carry you inside it. There you would perch on the motor cover next to the driver's seat and watch out the windshield every mile of the way drooling and panting in fear, but refusing to move away from your "watching spot". You sat like that for thousands of miles as we drove back and forth to Texas from Alaska and then as we went around Alaska on our little weekend campground jaunts.

Upon arrival anywhere you would hop out and circle the area deciding where it was safe for the children to play. And no stranger or other dog was allowed within that space until you carefully inspected them and gave your approval.

I could go on and on about all the ways you stayed faithful to us, even after that brain tumor took away so many of your skills and abilities. Even when you had no idea how to walk in a straight line and would get stuck nose first in a corner or a bush. There you would stand patiently until someone would find you and turn you around. That went on for so long that the kids and I knew that the end was near. You were incontinent and could no longer climb up the stairs to be with us at night. That's when I moved downstairs to help you and to sleep next to your blanket because you did not want to be left alone down there.

We were prepared to keep on this way as long as you didn't seem to be suffering anything but loss of dignity, but one evening as we sat down to eat, you suddenly began to scream in a way I

had never heard anyone scream before. You were obviously in terrible pain, and we could not delay the inevitable any longer.

I held you in my arms all the way to the emergency animal hospital, and you kept screaming as you looked up at me in your pain and fear. I held you close to me while the vet prepared his needle, and I told you over and over how much I loved you and that you were going to be fine, just fine -—and you were. One moment you were crying and rigid with pain, and the next second you went limp and silent in my arms. No more pain, no more fear.

We took you home wrapped in your blanket. Erik dug a grave in our backyard where you lie today, forty-three years after you came into our lives and showed us how to give love without asking for anything in return.

RING TUM DITTY

Now I ask you—who could resist a recipe called Ring Tum Ditty? Certainly, I couldn't, and I was so very, very proud when I learned how to fix it at my first Girl Scout camp experience.

I was eight-years-old, and I could hardly wait to get home so I could list the ingredients for Mom to buy because I wanted to make it all by myself for the family.

As the oldest child—and a girl at that—it was my expected duty to help my mother anytime she was in the kitchen. I still have the sprinkle little burn scars along my arm from the bacon grease popping up on me as I helped cook the family breakfast. And I can cook a delicious cream gravy from the beef or chicken crispies left in the supper skillet each night. I learned to stir them together with just the right amount of flour, salt and pepper until the flour is browned. Then milk is added and stirred carefully until gravy appears. It's magic!

But in our kitchen Mom made magic every day, and even though we did not have much money or a fine home, we certainly ate like rich folks! You see, when my daddy was young, there was such a severe food shortage in the dry cotton farming parts of west Texas where he grew up, that he recalled how some families in his county almost starved to death after World War I. He never forgot that and swore that his family would always have plenty of food – and we certainly did.

Even though we lived in Ft. Worth, Dad turned our single acre of land into a little farm all his own. We had a cow –a Guernsey because Guernsey cows produced the richest milk, and Dad did not want his children drinking "blue milk"— his name for the skimmed and pasteurized stuff. We had chickens and lots of eggs and fried chicken most every Sunday. We also had a yearling calf specially fattened up for us each spring by one of Dad's friends.

Once we even had a pig—my personal humiliation because no one—*no* one in our part of town ever had a pig in their backyard. And to make matters worse, this pig would sometimes escape from its pen and go squealing down the street with me chasing behind trying to turn it around with a stick. But revenge is sweet, and that winter I enjoyed plenty of bacon and other pieces of that ornery pig.

Daddy planted a huge garden every spring which he lovingly tended each evening when he came home from his daytime job as an engineer at General Dynamics.

Anyway, back to Ring Tum Ditty: In spite of the ribbing, I took from my younger siblings for its silly name, I started cooking it the next weekend with great ceremony. First, I cut up the onions—somehow, I hadn't noticed at camp how onions make you cry. Next the bacon had to be cooked in small pieces, and needed lots of stirring. Then I needed to add a can of corn. No problem, except I wasn't allowed to use the can opener yet, so I had to break my bragging promise to cook it all by myself. Mom graciously opened the can while I cut up the Velveeta, our cheese of choice in those days.

I tossed in the cheese chunks, stirred it all up and proudly served everything on pieces of toast made from our white, gummy bread. *Voila*! Mike had just cooked an entire meal for the whole family! And guess what—they loved it! In fact, Ring Tum Ditty became our family's default recipe until I went off to college.

Later I learned the family never ate Ring Tum Ditty again after I left, but that's another story.

POEMS:
I SAY ALASKA

When I say Alaska, you see ice and snow.
You see wild animals and big fish
Hauled out of cold, cold waters.
When I say Alaska, I see the rosy cheeks and little pink noses
of my three children.
Coming in from playing outside in the snow.
They peel off their wet snowsuits
and clamor happily for hot chocolate.
When I say Alaska, you see glaciers, mountains
And the calendar scenes of its unpeopled beauty.
I see that Alaska too – vast and empty and wild.
But I also see my home, warm and cozy
and full of my life.
I see my children, now grown and gone.
I see my friends smiling at one another in early spring
Congratulating each other for once again surviving
The cold, dark months of winter.
We know that long sunny days of summer lie ahead.
They are Alaska's gift to us for our winter toughness
And we don't want to miss an hour of their daylight.
We're now ready to plant our gardens,
Grow our flowers, and hike the wooded trails

That have been hidden under the snow all winter.
We have much to do, and there's no time to waste.
We know that summer will be over before we get it all done,
We also know we must use every bit of sunshine we can get
To store up the warm memories of Alaska's wild beauty
That will sustain us through another long, dark winter.

MY LEAST FAVORITE TIME OF THE DAY

The shadows are stretching dark and long
Across the road before me.
The sun seems done for the day.
It's gathering its light and leaving.
The air is cooling, the cicadas are calling,
But I'm feeling hollow inside.
It's my least favorite time of the day.

Once again, I haven't done what I set out to do
When the morning light was bright,
And the air was fresh and cool.
I knew just what I needed to do today and
I had a list to guide me.
But now it's long-shadow time again,
And my list is still not finished

So, I'll go fix dinner, have a glass of wine.
And start making my list for tomorrow.

NO RED HAT, PLEASE

You'd never know it looking at me now,
But not so long ago
I was fast moving and quick like a bunny,
As they say.
I was active, eager to go places and to try new things.
I was fearless, full of grit
And always on the go
But not these days.
No, now I'm slow, really slow.
I'm also tentative about new places
Or things to do.
I wobble when I walk, and let's face it,

I'm downright clumsy.
I'm scared of fast traffic,
Or driving in the dark.
And did I mention that I'm slow, really slow?

I CARRY MY MOTHER

I carry my mother inside me
I hear her words coming out of my mouth
I feel her fingers trying to smooth the errant cowlicks
I inherited from her.
I see her hands as I hold my book and turn the pages
I feel her longing deep in my loins as I watch a mother
cuddle her child.
I hear her voice telling me what to admire and what to spurn
And if I turn quickly enough,
I see her face in my mirror.

1/26/2012

daedalian

quarterly
fall 1956

REFLECTIONS IN BLACK AND WHITE

Mikell Murphy

On the lower shelf of the bookcase next to our living room mantel lies a small, black photograph album fondly labeled, "Mike's Birthday Pictures." I re-discovered it last summer while in a rare, but vigorous fever of house cleaning. It lay there almost buried amidst a pile of more imposing snapshot albums lovingly filled by my mother, not only to show off her darlings for personal enjoyment, but also to bestow upon posterity the illustrated story of "The Four Little *Unphotogenic* Murphys and How They Grew." Perhaps I was only hunting an excuse to end my dusting efforts, or perhaps I was actually curious about my appearance in the bygone days of baby fat and toothless grins. At any rate I reached for the little album and began slowly to thumb through it.

Page, one called for a second look. A curly-headed baby stranger sat in a monstrous high chair, staring with wild eyes at a lone, candle atop a very large cake. "Why, that's me!" I marveled. "Wonder what ever happened to the curly hair?"

My question did not go completely unanswered long, for the next photo supplied the date of the beginning of my present-day "naturally straight" hair. A pudgy infant was standing proudly beside a table which held a cake with two candles perched on its top. I am sure the cake and candles were not the reason for the snooty smile I was giving the birdie, however. It was rather plain that the real object of my affection was an over-sized bow somehow pasted on my otherwise unadorned pate. Something, I do not know what, happened in my second year which had drastic permanent effects on my curls.

Scene three in the birthday album took place in a different setting. The little, white table, the large, round cake, and the small, round girl were now standing together on a wilted lawn. The sun must have been hot enough to melt the cake's three candles (It always is at that time of the year in South Texas) for my twisted expression was plainly saying. "Let's get this foolishness over and move back inside." Even the spare shade of a nearby oil derrick—(my first conception of a tree)—was not helping the situation.

The fourth birthday must have been cooler, (or at least breezier, than the third, for I looked much more calm and patient than before. In fact, I looked completely nonchalant, and it was quite a sophisticated unexpected puff of wind had the audacity to stand my circular skirt perfectly straight out in front giving the whole world a glance at my frilly underwear. With a snicker I flipped the page.

At five I was the possessor of my first genuine boyfriend, and I insisted that Bert share the limelight with me at the white table. We stood there together smiling our most toothful smiles toward the box camera. I was in blissful ignorance of the fact that I was soon to part with both Bert and those baby teeth forever.

During that year we moved to Fort Worth, a complete change from the oil frontier of Duval County, and I paused before turning the page to remember some of my early opinions of the "big city." Most of them were based on Fort Worth's booming aircraft industry then at its wartime peak. For days after our arrival, I stood outside with my head thrown back and my mouth open in amazement as droning B-24's, the "Liberators" on their way over the world, barely cleared the telephone wires across the street. I had never laid eyes on an airplane before, so it took weeks for the novelty to wear off enough that I would give in to the crick in my neck and stop rushing outdoors at every sound of a motor in the sky.

For my sixth birthday Mother braided my hair in two stubby pigtails, and I stood again by the little table. This time the cake was especially dear to me, for a war was going on and sweets were hard to find. Besides, this cake was chocolate, my very favorite kind. My grin of approval exposed a dark gap in the front of my mouth. The fairies had made their first raid but had squared the deal by leaving a dime under my pillow.

By next year the pigtails were no longer stubby; they were long enough to let their perky bows bounce with each head toss. I was getting to be a big girl, and my attitude was quite condescending toward this fol-de-rol of birthday snapshots with cake and table. After all, I would soon be in the second grade and learn how to spell like Alicia, my friend across the street.

Pictures eight, nine, and ten were stairstep duplicates of one another. Each recorded my height, pigtail length, and growth of the shrubbery on the sunny west side of our home. View eleven was slightly different, however.

A chocolate cake was still sitting on a baby-sized table, but it was now beside a smiling youngster in a green Girl Scout uniform. I smiled as I remembered how thrilled I had been to have my birthday fall on my troop's meeting day. My friends had shouted the happy-birthday song in an off-key bellow that nevertheless fell on my ears with the softness of a harp solo. The pigtails were gone; the smile showed for the first time in years a full set of teeth. Here and there the beginning signs of an adolescent curve were visible. Yes, there had been many changes between the one-candle cake and the eleven-candle cake, and these little black and white reminders from the old box camera showed them to me more clearly than ever before.

Softly I closed the book and returned it to the shelf. Thoughtfully I went on with my dusting.

Happily, I continued to reflect on the good, full life of my childhood.

THE BLUE BUTTERFLY AND MY DEAD FRIEND

In Costa Rica Dave and I were always on the lookout for the beautiful blue morpho butterfly, the "mariposa azul." It is bigger than a big man's hand and it its iridescent electric blue wings shimmer in the sunlight. If it flies anywhere near you, you just cannot miss it–except you can and you usually do.

You see, the elusive blue morpho butterfly has a remarkable trick for hiding in plain sight. Though it's as obvious as a fluttering blue flag and vividly stands out against the trees and shadows of the jungle where it lives, it literally disappears as soon as one approaches it. Chase it and it dives into some secret hidey-hole you cannot see or find, and it stays there until you give up looking for it.

Then *poof!* It magically reappears, flashing its brilliant blue wings and leading you on in the chase to catch or capture its beauty. On and on, you search and follow its lead, but each time you approach, it again instantly disappears.

How does it do this, you wonder? And when you later find out, you want to smack your head at the simplicity of the answer. You see, the top side of the blue morpho is that sparkling bright blue that draws all eyes and cannot be missed, but the underside is drab brown and gray, the color of the surrounding jungle and a perfect camouflage.

The blue morpho is not hiding at all. It's still flying right in front of our eyes, but it is only showing us the ordinary colors of the world. And because we are so accustomed to looking at those, we really do not see them.

In its homeland, the blue morpho is the symbol of peace and happiness.

Remember this as I tell you about my friend who unexpectedly passed from this life a few days ago.

Rosanne was an amazing woman—an artist, an author, an adventuress. She was so funny, a great story teller, and an intrepid traveler. She hiked hundreds of miles across mountains, often alone, ran marathons, and earned advanced degrees in English and theology, while raising three successful sons to manhood. She was never frightened or reluctant to try something new, but she carefully avoided the common and ordinary sides of life.

Rosanne identified herself as a "seeker." She was always seeking answers to the questions she constantly asked about the meaning of life. She deemed herself a pilgrim and considered her life a pilgrimage toward her goals of inner peace and happiness.

She never got there in this lifetime. Some cruel and unknown entity attacked her brain and turned her from a strong and healthy woman into a helpless, bedridden invalid in just a few short weeks. She could never have stayed like that, however, so she soon escaped that fate and left this world.

It all happened so fast that it is hard to believe that she won't be calling any minute now to ask me again if I'm "at home and receiving" so that she can come over for a cup of coffee or a glass or two of wine. I miss her. I always will,

but I feel certain that she is now in a place where she has found the answers to all her questions.

Now she can see both sides of the blue morpho – and of life. So, I'm sure she realizes at last that peace and happiness are just the other side of our ordinary world. They are right here all along for us to see and to enjoy.

MY LOST HONEYMOON

"Hey! Wait a minute!" I want to scream.

"You've got the wrong bride here! This isn't the way my honeymoon is supposed to be! You told me we would tour Europe for six weeks and spend most of our time together in romantic Paris and Rome—my long-dreamed-of destination cities."

But here I am instead, jammed into a tiny Volkswagen sedan in Copenhagen, Denmark, with my new husband's really old mother and father whom I've just met and who don't speak enough English for us to really talk with each other. I'm still in shock since I just heard from my husband this morning that his "Mor and Far" had decided to ride along with us so they could get to know me better and could re-visit some of their favorite European cities along the way.

This was *not* at all the romantic honeymoon my smooth-talking Danish husband had been promising me for the last year and a half!

But here I am and here we go—off on my grand tour of Europe at last—just not exactly the tour this Texan girl had been dreaming about since high school. Even in my weirdest dreams I could not have come up with the strange experiences I would have this summer, the summer of my lost honeymoon.

It was 1961, the year of Erich Fromm's best-selling travel guide, _Europe on $5.00 a Day._ Jorgen, my new husband, had proudly handed me a copy on our flight from Alaska to Copenhagen. He explained how I would be our navigator and would find the best values in hotels and restaurants along the way by following the suggestions in this little book. He assured me that it held all the answers we would need.

To help us stay within our meager budget, Mor had packed lunches for the trip, a big can of ginger cookies, some boxes of stinky cheeses and crackers, along with a very large salami, some warm beers and a bottle of Danish Aquavite. I had already learned the hard way that Aquavite is an explosively strong alcoholic drink that can knock the top of your head off, especially if you drink it the Danish way– straight down the hatch in one gulp and then chased with swallows of beer.

With the smelly lunches finally stowed in Mor's big ba between my feet we were off with the three Danes arguing at the top of their lungs about which route to take and me, staring morosely out the back window feeling isolated and sorry for myself.

That night I stood up to Jorgen for the first - but certainly not the last - time in our marriage. I told him I would not ride in the back seat with his mother. I wanted to be up front next to him so we could at least talk together. This meant that his six-foot father had to squeeze into the backseat of that silly little car hour after hour, day after day occasionally moaning, "ohh, min bene, min bene!" I knew he was saying, "my legs, my legs"—but I was so bent out of shape by his unexpected presence on my "honeymoon" that I didn't sympathize, much less offer him my front seat again. After all, he was almost totally blind and couldn't see anything out the windows anyway. Besides, dammit! This was my honeymoon and I wasn't going to spend it trying to communicate day after day with my 70-year-old mother-in-law who only nodded and smiled and every ten minutes would offer me another ginger cookie.

Far had a strict schedule and a daily routine that we were all required to follow. After our cheese and cracker breakfast we would hit the road without stopping until far would open his Braille wristwatch and feel for the marks telling him the time. If it was anywhere near noon, we immediately pulled over. Mor would climb out and spread a cloth for the lunch she had packed —more salami, cheese and crackers—a little warm beer for Jorgen, a warm Fanta soda pop for Mor and me to split, and a small glass of Aquavite for Far. I soon realized that the Aquavite was the main reason we stopped each day. Both far and Mor declared that it was a medicinal requirement for Far, and who knows—maybe it was.

The noontime driving stop was also an opportunity for a potty break for all four of us. If we had stopped where there was no restroom nearby, far went right ahead and took care of his business. He would carefully walk about 25 steps away from the car and proceed to unzip and take a whiz. This was usually no problem, but when we were on the autobahn or some other busy road, it could get awkward because far could be right next to traffic but totally unaware of it. Mor would shush us because she knew he was too blind to understand the situation and she didn't want to embarrass him. I soon realized that Mor spent most of her time and energy protecting Far from embarrassment.

When we finally reached Paris, I was so excited I could hardly attend to my navigational duties for staring out at all the wonderful sights. Far insisted we stop right away at a bank so he could exchange his Danish krone for French francs. Only later did he realize that he had left his wallet and passport at the bank. Naturally the Danes flew into a loud panic blaming each other for forgetting not only the wallet and passport but also which bank where it had been left. As we drove around and around, it seemed that every bank in Paris was named National Bank of France, and they all looked alike. It took the rest of the day to find the one we needed, and that was how we spent the first of our two days in Paris. I was wondering why I had suffered through two years of college French classes with Mademoiselle Arbuthnot if this was how I was going to use what she had tried to teach me.

We were so hungry by evening we stumbled from one menu board to another along the street of restaurants where we found ourselves after sunset. Mor kept telling everyone that Far was so very hungry he needed to eat without further delay. Far would chime in to say that he was not particular about the menu or price– he was now so hungry he'd eat anything but *"kune mave"* (the Danish term for tripe, which is made from a cow's stomach). However, Jorgen insisted we stick to our $5 a day budget, so we had to keep walking. Finally, he found a menu and a restaurant that suited him. I wondered why he was grinning so broadly until I read on the menu board that the special for the day was tripe! Mor shook her head but Jorgen just hurriedly ushered us all in and told the waiter we would have the special of the day.

When it came, we dug right in. It had been a long time since lunch and the French chefs can work wonders, even with cow's stomach. Mor kept casting worried glances at Far as he sawed at his tripe. Jorgen had told him it was some French beef thing and now he slyly asked his dad how he liked his French dinner.

"It's OK," Far replied, "It might be French, but it tastes like *kune mave* to me." Blind as he was, he was not fooled by Jorgen's little joke.

So, Paris was a disappointment, but we were now headed south to Rome and Venice. My spirits rose as the weather felt warmer and the VW felt a little roomier. We had finally finished the salami, so it smelled better too.

But it was August in southern France, and the roads and villages we passed through were full of vacationing French folks. Far and Mor began to warn Jorgen that we'd better stop soon or we might have a problem getting a room for the night. Jorgen ignored them and kept asking me to find a hotel in our little guidebook that would fit our daily $5.00 budget. Unfortunately, we were now along the French Riviera and cheap hotels were not to be found in that area. In fact, a few miles down the road a little later, no hotels at all were to be found.

It grew dark. We were now in the rural countryside with no towns or villages anywhere to be seen. When we did come upon a country inn of some sort, Jorgen would stop the car and go inside, asking for a room. Then he would come back to us muttering in utter disgust that nothing was available.

It was quite late and very dark before he stopped by the road, shut off the engine, leaned back a bit, closed his eyes and went sound asleep! The oldsters and I couldn't believe it! Here we were, jammed into this little VW in the middle of nowhere, and Jorgen was asleep at the wheel— literally!

That was one of the longest nights in my memory. Far kept moaning about his legs being bent into cramps and Mor would lean forward, tap me on the shoulder, and in her most pitiful small voice say, "Little Mikell (she always called me little Mikell even though I was a full head taller than she was), Little Mikell, you must move over and start driving."

It was a crazy idea, but I would certainly have done it if I could have. In fact, I would have pushed Jorgen right out of the car and onto the roadside if I could have budged him from behind that steering wheel. I poked and pinched him, but he went right on peacefully snoring until daylight when he yawned, stretched, and innocently asked if anyone needed to get out and pee. Of course, we did, so we crawled stiffly from our captivity and prepared for another day. Far angrily criticized his son for our miserable night, but Jorgen did not seem to understand why we were upset and he certainly made no effort to apologize. He just kept driving toward Florence, Italy.

We left Far and Mor in Florence for two nights. They said it was because Florence was their favorite Italian city, but I was pretty sure they just wanted out of the VW. Who could blame them?

Jorgen and I had two nights to ourselves in Rome, and I was thrilled. Our $5.00 a day book led us to a tiny square with a breathtakingly elaborate fountain across from the hotel where we stayed. The hotel itself was not much to look at. In fact, it appeared to be really shabby with no glass in the windows on the third floor where our room was located. But that was fine with me because the fountain turned out to be the famous Trevi fountain, the same one that Audrey Hepburn had tossed her pennies into as the orchestra played "Three Coins in a

Fountain" in the movie of the same name. Audrey's wish had come true so I couldn't resist trying my luck with pennies too. Our room was directly across the narrow street from the famous fountain and high enough above it for me to be able to toss coin after coin into the water from our open window with no problem. So, I did!

The next day however, there was another miscommunication between Jorgen and me. None of our cheap rooms had bathrooms or showers in them. We had been on the road in the August heat long enough for me to badly need a shampoo and shower. Jorgen and I strolled around the streets after our inexpensive, but tasty, spaghetti lunch until we came to a little beauty salon. Jorgen left me there saying he'd be back in less than an hour, just time for a shampoo and set. He had our money, so he would pay when he returned and then we would go eat some fine Italian food somewhere close by.

I felt really luxurious for the next hour, but then I was ready to go. I sat waiting by the door for my husband to come get me and pay the nice ladies who had been so sweet to the Alaskan bride. But time continued to pass and no Jorgen appeared. I got worried. Maybe he had been run over by one of those terrible Rome drivers. Maybe he was lying in some Italian hospital somewhere and I needed to be with him. Maybe he had forgotten about me. The two little shop ladies fluttered around trying to keep me calm because I was obviously close to panic about my lost man.

Eventually they gave me a manicure to calm me down—still no Jorgen. Then they gave me a pedicure—my first pedicure ever—and still no Jorgen. By now it was dark outside and all the other shops along the street were closed.

I didn't know what to do. I had no money and no idea what our hotel's name was and there was no phone in the shop even if I had known the hotel's number.

The sweet little shop ladies were hanging in there with me, but they were obviously losing patience. They still wanted to help, but they'd run out of things to do with me and besides, I had run up quite a bill and Jorgen had the money. So we were all stuck. It was another long hour before Jorgen ambled in looking sheepish and sleepy.

Yes, he had fallen asleep for a little nap back in the hotel room and had overslept. I was so thankful that he was not dead or injured that I forgot how upset I had been at him and was actually glad to see him at last. And the little shop ladies rejoiced along with me at his return. I thanked them profusely, Jorgen paid the bill, and we left.

We finally found a small café still open, ate another dish of spaghetti, and went on strolling through the dimly lit streets and telling each other how lucky we were to actually be in Rome together—just the two of us.

After collecting Far and Mor from Florence, we headed to Venice, the next stop on our grand tour of Europe. In those days you had to park your car outside the storied city of canals and then use the phone to make a room reservation from a list of approved hotels before you could ride the Vaporetto into the city itself. The Vaporetto is a large water taxi —sort of like a big water bus, and it delivered us right to our hotel's watery front door.

I had made it absolutely clear to Jorgen from the phone booth area that this time I insisted on having a room with a shower in it. I was tired of sharing one with all the other people on the hotel floor. He promised he had reserved a very large room with a shower for us, even though we had to share it with his parents.

Oh well, nothing is ever perfect, is it?

When we had lugged our bags up the stairs to the third floor and opened the door to our room, there it was as promised—a large room with a bed in each of its four corners and in the center of the room was the promised shower stall. It turned out to be a metal container with a plastic curtain around it sitting on the floor right in the middle of the room. At that point I quit making demands and asking for what I wanted on this trip. I just relaxed - sort of - and went with the flow of my lost honeymoon which lasted for three more long weeks.

MY LIFE AS A DRUGGIE

Slowly my eyes opened wide enough to squint into the darkness around me. I was in a strange room all alone in a strange bed hearing strange voices outside my door. They were talking and laughing among themselves, obviously having a party without even inviting me to join them.

I tried to call for husband Dave, but my throat was too sore to croak out his name. I could feel that he was not in bed next to me where he belonged, so I intended to give him a piece of my mind for not including me in the fun going on outside the door.

This is nuts, I thought. I'll go out there myself. I tried to sit up but I was all tangled in lines that held my legs to the mattress, my pointer finger to the side of the bed, and my throat to a small plastic bag taped to my collarbone. I decided I'd have to free myself before I could get up and go, so I got busy yanking on the finger attachment first. I needed that hand to undo the leg lines.

But before I could even start loosening the leg lines, Barb, my very large night nurse, hurried in and pushed me back down onto the bed, "What do you think you're doing? You're not even supposed to be trying to sit up!"

"I want to get up and go out where they're having a good time, "I calmly explained. "And where's my husband anyway?"

"Nobody's having a good time, and your husband is at home, so lie down and go back to sleep."

She out all the lights and shut the door firmly, leaving me to fume alone in the darkness. This definitely has added insult to injury. First of all, I hurt everywhere and now I'm being left out of the fun. I will not stand for this! Where am I anyway? The furniture is different and the walls don't have our kids' pictures on them. I am looking out of an unfamiliar wall of windows showing dark mountains silhouetted against a pale night sky. What's going on?

I have come up with a plan. I have learned that if I press the button on my bed some nurse somewhere will respond and ask me over a little speaker what I need. If I say that I need to go to the bathroom the nurse will always say that she will be right in to help me. By now I know she will not be in right away, but she will appear eventually and then I will ask her to unfasten the lines holding me down and to help me get of bed.

And that's what happens, except that instead of an unknown nurse, it is big Barb who appears at my bedside again. She silently unfastens all my lines and tubes and helps me sit up on the edge of the bed preparing to take me to the bathroom. That's when I say, as assertively as I can manage, "Now, take me to that chair by the window so I can sit and look out at the mountains like a normal person."

Barb doesn't like the idea, but I get louder so she calls for reinforcements as she half carries me across the little room. In strides Eric, a truly big male nurse I don't know.

Barb explains to him, "She won't stay in her bed and insisted I get her over here by the window so she can look out at the mountains."

"Like a normal person ", I chime in. "And now please bring me my newspaper and cup of coffee."

Barb and Eric look at me as if I am crazy. "Look, you just got out of major surgery a few hours ago, so you need to be in bed."

"I NEED to look out at the mountains while the sun comes up. I *need* to read my morning paper and drink my coffee like a normal person the way I do every morning," I say.

Eric tries to reason with me. "We don't have a morning paper for you.

"Yes, you do. It's on the front porch right by the door. Just get it and bring it to me. And I like my coffee black."

"Look, we're on the seventh floor of the hospital and we don't have a front porch."

"Of course, you do. Everybody has a front porch. Just open the door and pick up the paper lying there," I insist.

Barb has already left, having given up on making me behave like a good little patient. Eric shakes his head and also walks out muttering while I try to get comfortable in this strange chair.

After a short while Eric returns, smacking a rolled-up newspaper on his open palm with a funny look on his face. "Here's your paper, "he says wearily.

"Thank you", I say politely. "And now, where's my coffee?"

Eric sighs, rolls his eyes and says, slowly, "We're making it now."

So, I settle down with my coffee and newspaper to enjoy the sun coming up over the mountains outside my window—just like a normal person.

Later I found out that I had been given two hydrocodone tablets at bedtime for the after-surgery pain. I had never had much medication before, so it must have hit me harder than expected. Actually, I enjoyed the affects while they lasted that day. I liked the way they made me feel like a queen with my very own minions who had to obey me.

MY CREDO

Several times over the years I have tried to put down on paper my credo, the belief that guides my life, but so far I have not completed a single one of those efforts.

I can explain my theories about a good life and what happens when we die—no heaven or hell but the re-joining of my spirit with the universal presence of light and love and other spirits. However, I have never been able to put into words my explanation of "God".

Long ago I gave up the idea of the bearded man on a throne in the sky, but I haven't yet replaced that childhood vision with another one that makes better sense to me. I do know there is a god because I talk to God every day. I am either pleading for guidance and help or else saying thank you, thank you, thank you for whatever it is I'm enjoying or appreciating at the moment. I *need* God all the time and everywhere; therefore, my credo must have a God in it who is truly omnipotent and omnipresent.

My God is totally inclusive. That means anyone who tries to put a boundary around who God loves or does or does not love; anyone who says certain people are not going to have the same chance at everlasting life as everyone else is not talking about the God I know. No one and no place can be excluded from my God!

As part of the "Building Your Own Theology" class at the local Unitarian Universalist Church of the Hill Country we wrote our own personal ethical ten commandments. This exercise took many hours of sorting through my beliefs about what is important to me and then distilling them into just ten statements to guide my life. Here they are:

1. Be kind to others and to yourself.
2. Be honest and trustworthy.
3. Love others in your life even when they are not being lovable.
4. Use words and language that will not hurt others.
5. Be glad for what you have instead of wanting more.
6. Take good care of your body.
7. Take good care of our Earth.
8. Take special care of children.
9. Work toward peaceful solutions when conflict occurs.
10. Use your time as if it is limited, for indeed it is.

So here it is—my credo. It will probably change as the years change me, but at least it is finally down on paper!

MOM WANTED "MORE"

The last time I sat next to Mom that summer as she faded away from us, she suddenly startled me out of my doze. She lifted her head and stared straight ahead. With a wild-eyed gaze she declared clearly, "I should have had more!"

Then she sank back down into her usual curled posture of fatigue and defeat and returned to staring blankly at her folded hands.

"What, Mom, what?" I turned quickly so that I could see her face.

"More what, Mom? More babies? More time with Dad? What did you want more of? Was it money? Did you want more money?"

Lord knows, no matter how Mom and Dad scrimped and saved we always needed more money than Dad could bring home from his hated job out at "the plant." But Mom could not rise again from that mental miasma which held her captive those last years, so I was never able to find out what she meant by "More."

I do believe that there are women who find satisfaction and contentment with their lives no matter how ordinary they are, but Mom was not one of them. Dad adored her and worked to please her with every breath he drew.

Together they raised four bright and healthy children whose highest ambition was to make Mom and Dad proud. But somehow Mom plodded through her days needing "more." It was never spoken but was always there – some vague heaviness we could sense beneath the surface but could not identify or change.

Mom died a few months later that summer and has been gone for years now, but I still miss her badly every day and I still wonder—What was it she wanted more of? What would have made her actually happy?

January 1933

DAD'S WORLD VIEW

My dad, Big Hank Murphy, was the best dad a girl could ever have. He was a gentle giant, the kindest, sweetest, most generous man you could ever meet. He was also a racist.

He never knew that, however. He was just a product of his time and upbringing on a West Texas farm. As he often said, he believed black folks were fine people—as long as they stayed in their place. He used the n-word till his dying day in spite of the embarrassment and protests of his four grown children.

Dad never knew a black person—and neither did I. They lived in a separate part of town, went to different schools, shopped in different stores, obviously drank from different water fountains and used different restrooms. And none of these differences ever seemed strange or unfair to me, I am ashamed to admit. I didn't know there could be any other way of living in Texas or the South. After all, I had never been anywhere else –and this was before TV or the internet's round the clock media coverage of news events. Our elementary school's big fund raiser was an old-fashioned Minstrel Show starring some prominent parents of our neighborhood in blackface and white gloves. The audience thought it was hilarious.

My favorite book was *Gone with the Wind*, which made slavery sound caring and benign. My high school US History textbooks and teachers taught us how the War Between the States was fought to protect our precious "states' rights" against the despotic federal government to the North. Years later in graduate classes at the University of Alaska I was amazed to learn that slavery was a major cause of the Civil War. Who knew?!

After college I quickly left Texas and headed all the way north to Alaska. There I was shocked to find I would have a few African American children in my 5th grade class. Even more surprising, the excellent teacher in the room next to mine was a wonderful black woman teacher. I learned a lot from her that year, and she was my first black friend.

Soon after arriving in Alaska, I was offered the chance to fly with a USO group all the way out to a big Naval Base on the Aleutian Island of Adak, a thousand miles from Anchorage. We were to entertain our "boys in blue" stationed there. This meant we were to attend a dance being planned for them. Sure enough, that evening a young black sailor asked me to dance with him. The whole time I was in his arms I was very worried about what Daddy would do if he could see me there. For sure he would come crashing through the doors and drag me back to Texas.

Years pass and the world changes—sort of—thanks to the Civil Rights movement and desegregation laws. My daddy would now have a hard time accepting all the black people living and working alongside us, starring on TV shows, winning on sports teams, or openly dating and marrying whites.

He would understand nothing of all this. He would be shocked and unable to grasp the reasons for the racial frustrations and festering anger that have erupted so recently in places where black people rise up against the unfair ways they are viewed or treated by the white police and the judicial system.

In Daddy's opinion black people should instead be grateful for all the progress they have made in the last 50 years. In Daddy's opinion the racial status was just fine the way it used to be. And unfortunately, my daddy's opinion is shared today by so many in America like him—the ones who have never really travelled far from home or experienced life with people who look different from them. How sad for us all!

Dad — 1934

AUNT EUNICE WAS A CLIFFT GIRL

Mom was the baby girl in a family of five girls growing up in Carrizo Springs, a dusty little town very near the Mexican border in far south Texas.

The girls' father, Andrew Clifft, was elected the first Mayor of Carrizo, as it was usually called. Even though his local importance had faded, folks still recognized his daughters as the "Clifft girls" while they grew up trying to find lives for themselves and a way out of Carrizo Springs. They fascinated me.

Even their names were intriguing: Florence Eunice, the oldest and toughest, Gladys Adelle, the fragile loner, Constance Audrey, the image-conscious flirt, Annie Maude, smiling sweetly through her meanness, and Burnice Ruth, the baby and our mother. Yes, her name was spelled "Burnice" not Bernice, and mother never liked it at all. Each name is a juxtaposition of longed for elegance and accidental clunkiness. They should have spawned a flock of youngsters who could have brought some resolution and healing to the family's fussing and feuding, but they didn't.

The Clifft girls L to R Maude, Audrey, Burnice (our mom), Eunice, Gladys

Dad and Mom -- 1934

Their marriage was a lifelong love match that produced four babies, myself, my two sisters, Sharon and Margwen, and our brother Don. We all grew up knowing we were loved and cherished by both parents. However, the other four Clifft girls did not have the same good luck as our mom did.

Aunt Eunice never had it easy. Life started out hard for her and stayed that way right up to the bitter, painful end. She was born prematurely, too early and too little. Curious neighbors and absolute strangers came to see the tiny baby. Grandma Clifft was still a teenager herself but was determined to save her little firstborn, so she kept Aunt Eunice wrapped up tightly in small box inside the warming oven of her kitchen cook stove.

The temperature much have been fine because Aunt Eunice not only survived but grew into a strong and hefty woman who could handle anything or anyone who got in her way—until cancer came along.

Aunt Eunice married our Uncle Alley Lansford, a lean and lanky ranch foreman who could have posed for the Marlboro Man ads except that he rolled his own Bull Durhams. We could hear his boots clomping and his spurs jingling all the way from the front door back to the kitchen where we eagerly waited for him. He smelled like horses and smoke, but we loved being close to him anyway.

Uncle Alley was not a very good-looking man. His face was nearly as long as some of his horses, and his teeth were yellow from the cigarettes that he would carefully construct while we watched in fascination. As he slowly drawled out some bit of news about his day on the ranch, he would remove the Bull Durham bag of tobacco from his shirt pocket, take out a cigarette paper and carefully form it into a little trough between his thumb and forefinger. Then he would use his teeth to pull the strings at the top of the tobacco bag to open it. After he had shaken out just the right amount of the golden-brown shreds of tobacco to fill his furled paper, he'd use his teeth again to pull the strings and close the bag so he could put it back into his pocket. He would then lick the paper all along one edge and roll the whole little mess into a surprisingly regular-looking cigarette. Uncle Alley would twist one end to close it and stick it between his sunburned lips while taking a match from some other pocket. Next would come the part we had been waiting for. He would flick the match head with his thumbnail and hold its flame to the limp cigarette dangling from his lips producing a sudden flare-up of tobacco and paper that was truly impressive. Only by tilting his big head way over to the side did Uncle Alley escape torching his nose hairs.

We also enjoyed watching Uncle Alley drink his coffee while he smoked what was left of his cigarette. In those days everyone used a cup and saucer to serve coffee. Uncle Alley would pour a little out of his cup and into his saucer which he would then pick up, blow on, and slurp from. Watching Uncle Alley have his morning coffee and a cigarette was entertainment indeed for us!

When he was much younger, a horse had thrown Uncle Alley, and he had landed on his head. He lay in a coma at home for a long time. Stories vary about how long, from days to weeks to months, but it was generally agreed that he would have died for sure except for the excellent care he got from Aunt Eunice.

However, when he woke up again, Uncle Alley was a drinking man. Why not, I always wondered? After all, the guy must have had a horrible headache, and Aunt Eunice was not one to bother with anyone's pain or to come running with an aspirin.

In spite of his problem with alcohol, Uncle Alley remained everybody's friend, a lovable guy and an excellent cowboy. He would have been a great daddy too if Aunt Eunice had not been so firm with her Clifft girl no-baby policy. He thoroughly enjoyed Sharon and me whenever we visited Carrizo Springs.

One summer day Uncle Alley decided to take us downtown for a soda pop as a special treat. We had never been anywhere alone with him and were very excited. Off we went to the town square, a collection of shops and cafes that surrounded the county courthouse less than half a mile from the Clifft home. We would enter a place and be greeted enthusiastically by all its occupants as Uncle Alley proudly showed us off and bought us each a soda pop. When we finished, we would go with him to the next place and the scene would be repeated. As the afternoon wore on, we made our way around the town square drinking more soda pops than we had drunk in our entire lives. We were fawned over by Uncle Alley's many friends, and thoroughly enjoyed being the center of attention.

We were having a wonderful time until the bar's swinging doors flew open and through the smoky haze, we saw Mama and Aunt Eunice bearing down on us not looking happy at all. Things got very quiet in a hurry. Mama yanked us off our stools. Out the door we went while Aunt Eunice collared Uncle Alley. We all hustled home in a grim silence.

Only later did we learn that Uncle Alley had taken us to every bar on the square and that while we drank our sodas, he was drinking his beers. I only hope that the good time we had together with him that day was worth the trouble he was in because of it.

During his years as a cowboy Uncle Alley was foreman on some huge ranches in South Texas. I only remember the names of San Pedro and Dentonia, each spread over several thousand acres in a land so barren that it required many acres to sustain each cow.

One day Uncle Alley took Sharon and me with him as he rode out to look over the cattle herd in some distant corner of the prickly pear and mesquite acreage he supervised. We went in style! He drove us in a black buggy drawn by a high stepping horse for miles until we came to one of his "line camps." There we pulled up to a campfire where a wizened little brown man was stirring a big pot of beans and guarding a pan of biscuits from the cowboys lounging around him and his green chuck wagon. Nearby was a three-sided lean-to with a straw roof and dirt floor where one of the cowboys obviously lived with his family.

In those days before green cards and border patrols many of the ranch hands in that part of Texas were "wetbacks." They had come across the Rio Grande from Mexico illegally, were grateful to be working in Texas, and Texans were glad to have them working on their ranches and farms.

Uncle Alley helped us down from the buggy, and then we saw why he wanted to show us this particular camp. Out of the straw-roofed shelter came running a lovely little Mexican girl, just our size, and maybe our age. Her name was Ramona and she was thrilled to see other little girls way out there in the middle of nowhere. We followed her inside the cool shade of the lean-to as she chattered happily in Spanish.

She proudly showed us to her mother who was quietly stirring a bowl of some kind of mush as she sat next to a cradle hanging from the ceiling. Ramona leaned over the cradle's rim and gently touched the baby sleeping inside it. Then she straightened up again, and we went outside with her to run around the camp together pretending we knew what we were all talking about.

Ramona had a little cloth baby doll that she let us hold and a little tin cup she pretended the doll could drink from. Ramona also had pierced ears with little gold earrings that fascinated Sharon and me. Pierced ears were so lovely but forbidden to us! Only Mexican girls could have pierced ears, you know. And that's what we believed implicitly until we were middle-aged women and finally felt rebellious enough to get our ears pierced.

The afternoon passed too quickly and we soon were back in the buggy with Uncle Alley bouncing over the miles to the ranch house. For years afterward Sharon and I would talk enviously about the happy, carefree life Ramona must have had—a house with only three sides and open to the sun and the air, a baby that could swing from the ceiling, and earrings! Gold earrings! What a lucky girl that Ramona was!

While Uncle Alley was busy with the affairs of the ranches he managed, Aunt Eunice was left alone and isolated in a variety of ranch houses, each one different from the others except that they were all surrounded by miles of dry brush and prickly pear. She read every book she could find, studied the sky and animals around her and found other things to keep her busy. She gathered an amazing arrowhead collection she proudly displayed until some shameful thief stole it.

She loved animals and had a series of strange pets. I especially remember the razorback hog brought to her as a baby that she nursed to full-grown viciousness. That wild pig was devoted to Aunt Eunice and followed her around like a dog but would come barreling out of nowhere to attack anyone else. His tusks could sink through boot leather like a knife through warm butter. Folks learned in a hurry to stay inside the safety of their cars and to honk until Aunt Eunice came out to see what was happening. She would walk right up to that snarling, snapping beast and pick him up by the bristling hair along his spine. She was strong enough to hoist him up like a sack of flour and carry him to her little yard. With a few scolding words, she would fling him over its fence. Then she would turn and graciously welcome her guests.

Aunt Eunice also showed her tough streak during WWII when there were some old-fashioned range wars going on in the county over who could sell their land to the highest bidder the fastest. Uncle Alley and Aunt Eunice were obviously on the wrong side of the ongoing battles. One day as they were driving along a deserted road back to their place they were stopped and surrounded by some hired thugs who dragged them out of their car.

One of them held Aunt Eunice while the others began to beat and kick Uncle Alley. Aunt Eunice could not free herself from her captor to stop the attack, but she managed to reach back and stick her thumb into his eye and began to pry his eyeball right out of the socket. He was a tough customer though and did not let go until Aunt Eunice had his eyeball hanging down on his cheek. That was enough for the gang to stop stomping Uncle Alley and to beat a hasty retreat.

Aunt Eunice said later that she never would have believed that it would be so hard to get an eyeball out of someone's head!

It is just a good thing Aunt Eunice did not have a gun on her that day or she might have killed someone. She was an excellent shot and could shoot small objects out of a person's hand at scary distances. *Don't mess with Aunt Eunice!*

Later in life Aunt Eunice became a teacher. The ranch job was becoming too hard on Uncle Alley and money was even shorter than usual, so she began to teach in the local school. She did not have a college degree or teaching certificate, but no matter. It was right after WWII and teachers were desperately needed, especially in the wretchedly poor and overcrowded schools of rural south Texas.

Many Mexican children found themselves jammed into bare classrooms not knowing how to read, write, or how to speak English. It fell to Aunt Eunice to whip them into acceptable student behavior—and whip she did! "Miz Lansford" became known as a teacher who could definitely get results from all sorts of students, so she was routinely given the toughest cases, the biggest, baddest boys in the school. But once she got them into her classroom and they began to understand that she meant business, they did begin to change their behaviors, and they did begin to learn.

Every summer Aunt Eunice went back to school determined to get her teaching certificate— that piece of paper that would force the school administrators to pay her what other teachers were making and what she definitely was worth. Summer after summer she drove many miles over to Kingsville at the bottom of Texas to take classes at the college there. At last, she completed all requirements and graduated with the other students, most of them years younger than she.

By then Uncle Alley was no longer able to work at all, and Aunt Eunice was supporting him as well as Grandma and Granddad Clifft back in Carrizo Springs. Now she could finally begin to be paid a full teacher's salary! She had at last reached her goal of being a college graduate!

Uncle Alley

Aunt Eunice as a teacher

But less than two years later a little mole on her upper arm was diagnosed as malignant melanoma, and Aunt Eunice was dying of cancer. Tough as she was, this was a fight she could not win. Florence Eunice Clifft Lansford was never free of pain again and did not live to see another summer. She died an agonizing death, surrounded by her younger sisters who could not believe that the one who had always gone on ahead of them, the one who could handle anything thrown at her by the unkind places and times she lived in could be beaten. But she was.

Aunt Eunice and Uncle Alley -- 1935

PROUD TO BE AN AMERICAN — SORT OF

First of all, you must understand that I believe with my heart and soul that America is by far the best nation on this planet. There is nowhere else I would rather live than right here in the good old USofA! And do not forget that as you read the following.

I believe that America has been building up some pretty scary negative karma for the last 200 years. We have mistreated many of the people and all of the animals who got in our way as we marched across this land with our absolute belief in our manifest destiny—that we were Godsent to settle this continent from the Atlantic seaboard all the way to the Pacific Ocean.

Of course, we, as a people, did not always agree on what we wanted to do with the land once we had secured it for ourselves. Some wanted to plow and plant it. Others wanted to leave it for the animals they brought to it. And even the animal bringers did not always agree with one another about what to do with the unfarmed land. There were bitter fights and even wars between the cattle men and the sheep men. And those violent conflicts had to wait in line until the while men had totally shamed and destroyed the Indian people who had lived here throughout their long histories.

Yes, I know the Indians were ferocious and brutal in the defense of the land they believed was where they belonged because it had always been there for them to use. They were deservedly hated by the settlers moving West, but Indians never had a real chance, did they? We whites had the power and the determination to overcome them, and so we did. We did not stop until the Indians were totally vanquished and left without their land, their culture, or their pride. And we will pay the price for that victory for years to come.

But it is not only the Indians that we proud Americans have mistreated. Our negative karma will include the Japanese citizens and Alaskan natives we put into "protective" concentration camps during WWII, taking their land and possessions without any compensation. The Alaskan Natives, a peaceful and benign population, are still struggling to reclaim their personal identities and the culture they lost when the White Man moved in and "civilized" them.

Surely, however, our worst karmic payback will come from the cruel and barbarous years we allowed slavery to remain the law of the land. For more than 300 years we fostered a culture which treated men, women and children as property, not as human beings at all. We did not protect slaves from ruthless and savage masters who drove them like animals and refused to grant them the freedom to live a life of their own choosing. Is it any wonder that a sharp and painful division and a lack of trust still exists between the blacks and whites of America today? This remains a jagged and bleeding wound to our nation.

And we continue piling up more negative karma today. Our current emphasis on acquiring more possessions and money than we personally need means that we are using our energies and efforts to possess more of our Earth's available resources for ourselves instead of sharing what we have with the seriously needy folks all around us. Thus, we are creating a shameful two-level society of haves and have-nots. To be the richest and most powerful nation on Earth and yet refuse to feed our hungry children, to provide health and medical help for the sick and weak, or to assure that all families have a place to live and safe water to drink is a cosmic disgrace that will surely one day bring us down.

We move closer and closer to that cultural tipping point when some angry group or a wronged Samson will appear in our midst with the strength to pull down our temples and to destroy our culture of fun and feasting as described in the Old Testament. It must happen eventually because karma can be denied for only so long before it is re-balanced.

The "Daedalian" was the literary magazine published by the English Department at Texas Woman's University. Each year every Freshman was required to write an essay for it. The English faculty then read them all and selected ten papers to be published in that quarter's issue of the magazine. My entry, "Reflections in Black and White," was one of the ten chosen in 1956. Here it is:

Printed by Libri Plureos GmbH in Hamburg, Germany